W9-BTR-510

Gifts from Nature

Gifts from Nature

Matthew Mead

Photographs by Monica Buck Text with Jill Kirchner Simpson

CLARKSON POTTER/PUBLISHERS

NEW YORK

TO MY GRANDMOTHER, who inspired me in the beginning,

MY PARENTS, who have always supported my endeavors, and

JENNY AND HER GIRLS, who have helped me realize my dreams

and given me the space to make them come true. **M.G.M.**

PUBLISHER'S NOTE: This book contains projects using flowers, herbs, and other ingredients that, when mixed properly, are perfectly safe. However, certain of the contents may cause an allergic reaction in some individuals, so reasonable care in the preparations is advised.

Copyright © 1997 by Matthew Mead
Photographs copyright © 1997 by Monica Buck

All rights reserved. No part of this book may be reproduced or transmitted in any form or by any means, electronic or mechanical, including photocopying, recording, or by any information storage and retrieval system, without permission in writing from the publisher.

Published by Clarkson N. Potter/Publishers, 201 East 50th Street, New York, New York 10022. Member of the Crown Publishing Group.

Random House, Inc. New York, Toronto, London, Sydney, Auckland

http://www.randomhouse.com/

CLARKSON N. POTTER, POTTER, and colophon are trademarks of Clarkson N. Potter, Inc.

Printed in Hong Kong

Design by Constance Old

Library of Congress Cataloging-in-Publication Data
Mead, Matthew
Gifts from Nature / Matthew Mead; photographs by Monica Buck; text with Jill Kirchner Simpson.—1st edition
1. Nature craft. 2. Gifts. I. Kirchner Jill. II. Title.
TT157.M447 1997   97-17086
745.5—dc21   CIP

ISBN 0-517-70689-X

10 9 8 7 6 5 4 3 2 1

First Edition

Acknowledgments

I would like to thank everyone who made the dream of creating this book a reality, especially Monica Buck, whose sensitive eye and keen perception helped create such colorful and natural photographs, and Jill Kirchner Simpson, who supported and guided me through much of this project and helped in making this book say everything I wanted it to, clearly, concisely, and beautifully.

So many kind and helpful people have been there from the beginning: my entire family, especially my mother and father, who always knew I dreamed of producing a book and instilled in me the belief that all things are possible; Jenny, who smiled all through the production of the book and gave me all of her love, support, and enthusiasm; Michelle and Renee, who remained funny, inspiring, and composed, even when placed in front of the camera; my sister, who helped me with early story proposals and ideas when I was unable to pay her, and my brother, who over many years has created wonderful props for all of my projects.

There are many friends without whom this project would not have been possible: especially Emelie Tolley and Chris Mead, who provided the avenue for this book and answered my many questions along the way; Mary Emmerling, whose work inspired me from the start, and who gave me a chance to prove I was a capable stylist; and Melissa Crowley, who always offered great advice and words of encouragement; my assistant, Barbara Koppel, who is tirelessly energetic, enthusiastic, and always accomplishes all of the technical and difficult assignments we share with ease and style—you are the best; Leslie Camacho of Dillinger's Upholstery, who worked on deadline to create the fabrications I dreamed of—always fabulous, always perfect, and always on time; Paul Meyer, who kept everything, including my computer system, upgraded and efficient; Mary and Gordon Welch and their daughter, Lindsey Crane, who did everything from hosting dinner parties for the crew and cutting sheets of glass to posing for photographs and baking sugar cookies for our autumn picnic; Jacques and Paula Despres of Jacques Pastry, who helped me design the superb pastries and candies for the book; Scot, Sydney, and Colby Kenyon and the entire staff at The Lamp Shop, who created magnificent lamps and shades, and always accepted deadlines with smiles; Winton Desrosia and his gallery, who made last-minute frames and mats for all of the framing projects.

To great friends who have lent me their homes, their props, and their support: Martha Foley, Faye D. Foster, Sharon Bernier, Pam Mulsow, Wendy Hall, Carmella Carter, Marge McGann, Heather McClintock, Sandy and Gino Tetreault, Bruce and Audrey Gardener; Everett Aldrich of the Village Green for his insightful information on the lupine of SugarHill; Kate Kerivan and her gardens at Bungay Jar Bed and Breakfast; Robyn and Bob Cotton and their daughters, Emily, Jennifer, and Isabelle, who opened their home, their hearts, and their dining table to accommodate our crew; Maureen and Ron Oliver and Judy McMurry of Interior Additions, who allowed us to shoot in their homes and in their shop; the family at Caring Gifts, who always remained helpful and enthusiastic; the Souther family and their amazing seaglass collection; the staff of Capitol Paint and Wallpaper, for their brilliant color matching; my good friends Lorin Gross and Joe St. Pierre, who were always interested in this project and added such insightful design ideas.

At Clarkson Potter, thanks to: my editor, Katie Workman, who always showed enthusiasm and kept me working hard; Lauren Shakely, who saw a book in my future and knew Katie and I would work well together; Erica Youngren, Andrea Peabbles, and Joy Sikorski for all of their diligent assistance; Howard Klein, who helped me find the best photographer possible; Robbin Gourley and Jane Treuhaft for their sensitive art direction; and Constance Old, for her remarkable talent and superb design of this book.

To all of you, this work has been a collaborative effort of which we should all be proud.

Contents

Preface

As a child, I remember collecting bright stems of goldenrod at summer's end to braid into harvest wreaths. Every year my family would drive around the countryside, walking the meadows to pick wildflowers to dry. The flowers were free for the taking—all we invested was time spent together in the out-of-doors. From my sister, I learned to celebrate the first hints of spring. She always filled tiny cold cream jars and bottles with whatever wildflowers she could find in the yard, and they were some of the most spectacular miniature arrangements I had ever seen.

My mother instigated my first foray into foraging: she equipped me with a coffee can and sent me searching for wild strawberries on a hillside we used in winter for sledding. I returned with a can full of bright red berries and a bright red sunburn to match. We sprinkled sweet handfuls over cream-filled biscuits and bowls of cornflakes. I picked ferns in the woods to create bouquets for mock weddings—a ritual that usually preceded playing "house." It wasn't until just a few years ago that I began to rediscover the ferns in the wild that I remembered gathering in my youth.

Today I continue to be fascinated by the seasons and nature's ever-changing offerings throughout the year—a bouquet of wild violets in springtime, the intricate fronds of a graceful summer fern, a carpet of colorful fall leaves under my feet, and the tickle of winter's first snowflakes as they melt on my face. The passage of the seasons is somehow always new and astounding, while also being comforting and familiar.

As I wrote this book, I walked meadows, hiked forests, and searched roadsides for flowers, ferns, stones, and grasses. I rethought my approach to gardening and flower arranging, focusing more on indigenous shapes and textures rather than artificially propagated colors and blooms. I foraged for fiddlehead ferns to create a meal and collected wild berries for summertime desserts. I devised recipes to create naturally soothing bath salts and scented soaps, and created everlasting Christmas decorations from unlikely seashore finds.

There is an amazing range of ways to explore our natural world—from decorating and crafting to simply observing and learning about the many species of native plants and flowers. I hope that reading this book will help open your eyes to some of the many gifts of nature.

Introduction

For many of us, nature has become sadly more and more removed from our daily experience—something to be visited on vacation or admired in photographs, but all too rarely savored as an integral part of our daily lives. We drive to the florist's to buy bouquets while beautiful wild-flowers, ferns, and foliage grow in our backyards and along our roads. Conditioned to view dande-lions as pesky weeds, we've forgotten or never known how pungent the greens taste in a salad. We buy elaborate Christmas decorations that must be stored in closets most of the year instead of borrowing from nature's riches to embellish our homes. And we've lost the ability or inclination to really see what's around us—the violets that springs up around the house; the willowy native grasses, beautiful in their unmanicured state, that can save us the constant labor of mowing a square patch of lawn; the wild berries that taste far better than anything found in a store.

Filled with simple, accessible ideas for bringing the beauty of nature into your home, this book is designed to encourage you to rediscover the many ways nature can enrich your day-to-day life. You'll find a wealth of artistic ways to use the earth's bounty in its natural state, from pressing and framing ferns to using shells as drawer pulls and candleholders. There are recipes to help you savor the fruits of foraging in the wild, and table setting and entertaining ideas that let nature set the theme. Other ideas are designed to enhance the sensory pleasures of nature, such as making your own pine-scented soap or violet bath water.

You'll find a field journal at the back of the book in which to chronicle your finds, as well as helpful lists of edible plants, endangered species, and ways to safeguard your well-being in the outdoors. You'll find suggestions for wildflowers, trees, berries, and cones easily collected and preserved for crafting projects; a list of rare and endangered plants that should be admired in their environment; and also a guide to land con-servancies, state forests, and botanical gardens that are open to the public and directories of mail-order sources for craft supplies and stores that feature unusual or rare natural finds.

Anything found in nature has a beauty all its own that requires little or no adaptation to be enjoyed. The natural world requires no money or special skills to be appreciated and is often as close by as your backyard. This world is, by and large, still available to us for the asking, if we use it respectfully and wisely.

Nature is an extraordinary gift—one that is perennially given to us, and one that we can give and share with others.

It seems as if winter may never end, and then suddenly, one day, small BUDS of green emerge from the TREES and fresh blades of GRASS start to push their way up through the CHILLED crust of earth. The sun's embrace becomes WARMER and the days start to stretch with added minutes of LIGHT. The air is sweetly tinged with FLOWERS and the pungent scent of fresh EARTH. Screens replace storm windows, letting the FRAGRANCE of spring waft through the house. A walk through the woods uncovers new GROWTH each day—the unfurling of FERNS, the blooming of flowers, the formation of buds ready to pop with downy NEW LEAVES. Spring is a short season, so one must learn to SAVOR its beauty: gather branches for forcing, collect woodland VIOLETS to decorate the table, and forage the meadows and roadsides for edible greens. The world is again filled with FRESH possibilities.

ON A WALK Spring is a time for the rejuvenation of the senses. Melting snow starts the melody of trickling water. The sun seems to intensify the newly emerging colors and embrace our bodies with warmth. The damp earth releases a distinctive scent of freshness. It is a time when a simple stroll can draw you close to the rebirth of nature.

DELICATELY UNFURLING FERNS

Along a country roadside, tall and lanky fiddle-head ferns rise from the ground. Right now they look like ordinary flower stems, yet soon their tightly wound ends will unfurl into a multitude of symmetrical bracts. Ferns are actually very primitive plants, some of the oldest remaining species on earth. I like to go in search of them in spring and take a few early cuttings to force in glass bottles at home. It is captivating to watch the leaves stretch open into lush and beautiful fronds.

LEFT Royal ferns grow leafy fronds ranging in heights of four to five feet. CENTER Sensitive fern grows in moist marshy areas, creating showy leaves and sprout pods. BELOW Within a tiny and tightly wrapped sprouting fern are the beginnings of eighteen to twenty symmetrical leaf formations. OPPOSITE Early cuttings of hay-scented ferns unfold their leafy bracts in water-filled bottles. A black-and-white plate from an antique book on fern identification is sealed between two pieces of glass as art and handy reference.

ABOVE This Art Deco urn is filled with living moss and placed on display in an old-glass dentists' cabinet.
OPPOSITE A flowering beech creates a spectacular tuft of white blooms similar to hydrangea blossoms.

FIRST SIGNS

Gather green velvety moss after the last snow has melted to create a beautiful token of spring. Fill an urn with a layer of stones, then potting soil, and place moss on top. Mist daily.

FORCING FLOWERS AND BRANCHES

There is a delicacy to even the trees in this season. The waxy sheen of freshly emerging buds captures the light; the new growth of a forest erupts into a brilliant canopy of chartreuse—a color that seems almost unique to springtime. I begin bringing the season inside as soon as possible, cutting branches that can be placed in water and coaxed into performing their seasonal magic indoors. Although branches from flowering trees and bushes such as forsythia and quince are most frequently used for forcing, any type of tree, whether flowering or not, can be forced (see "Field Guide," page 116, for a list of trees suitable for forcing). Forcing new green buds and leaves can be a subtle and refreshing change from showy flowers. Maple trees produce miniature chartreuse leaves, while other varieties, such as birch, sprout normal-size foliage. Forcing branches is a dramatic way to witness the unfolding spectacle of spring firsthand.

How to Force Branches

1 Cut the branches on an angle just above the nub where a branch would sprout. Use a sharp knife or pruning shears.

2 Place the branches directly into a basin of luke-warm water.

3 Make sure the vase or container has been cleaned thoroughly with bleach.

4 Fill the vase with a mixture of half fresh water, half tonic water.

5 Check the water every two days, and replenish it as needed. Change the water. if it becomes cloudy.

6 For best results, place the branches in a cool spot (no warmer than 60°F.).

SPRING WILDFLOWERS

The beauty of spring is expressed most unabashedly in flowers. Venturing out to search for them in country meadows, beside a stream, or even in the yard is almost always rewarded with handfuls of charming, delicate blooms. Some wildflowers, such as *bluets* (right), are found in moist, mossy patches in meadows or fields. They can be dug up in clumps and distinctively displayed, roots and all, on plates or in compotes. As long as you keep them by a sunny window and water regularly, they'll continue to grow and bloom for several weeks. Cheerful yellow *marsh marigolds* (left) can be found in early spring in the damp soil around a brook or stream. They add brilliant color to a window that looks out on a world awakening to green. Other flowers such as common *dandelions* or *wild mustard* often grow right in the yard, and make humble yet charming arrangements (below).

SENSORY PLEASURES: SPRING SCENTS

We often smell the freshness of spring as much as we see it: The warmth of the sun and the air release all the fragrances of the natural world coming to life. This is a wonderful time to walk outside and deeply inhale the fresh air we've missed for so long, being cooped up indoors. Relish the scent of:

- The air just before it rains, and just after

- Newly cut grass

- The delicate perfume of violets

- The salt-tinged moisture of seaside breezes

- Fresh earth, as the snow melts

- The fragrance of the pine-needle carpet blanketing the forest floor, as you trample upon it

- The damp richness of woodland moss

FORAGING FOR FOOD

Searching for food in nature, rather than in the aisles of the grocery store, may seem like an alien concept in today's convenience-food world, yet at one time Native Americans and others lived off the land, digging up edible roots, gathering wild greens, and picking berries in forests and fields. Even today, foraging for foods (those that grow naturally in the wild, rather than those farmed from seed) can be as simple as unearthing dandelion greens or fiddlehead ferns in your yard and then savoring their fresh-picked flavor in dishes such as Dandelion Green Pesto and Fiddlehead au Gratin (page 22).

Spring plants for foraging can usually be found at the edge of the woods in a shady area, in meadows and even lawns, by rivers an streambeds, or growing in woodlands. Though many of these plants also grow deep in forests, it is often easiest to identify them along a path, at the edge of a clearing, or beside a riverbank.

Guidelines for Foraging

1 Make sure the plants or flowers that you are gathering are not endangered species (see page 114).

2 Gather edible plants in open meadows and fields; avoid growth directly alongside a road, which accumulates toxins from the exhaust of passing cars.

3 Never eat a plant that you have not first identified in a guidebook of edible plants. These are available in libraries, bookstores, and hiking and outdoors stores.

4 If there is any doubt about the proper identification of a plant, DO NOT EAT IT. It is far better to pass up a questionable plant than to suffer the consequences of ingesting poison.

5 Plants should be foraged only from lawns that have not been chemically treated with insecticide.

6 Collect wild greens in early spring—more mature plants become tougher and less tasty.

7 Wash all plants thoroughly under cold running water.

DANDELION GREEN PESTO

A mixture of Italian cheeses, walnuts, oil, and dandelion greens creates a light and flavorful toss for pasta.

4 cups fresh young dandelion leaves, washed
3 garlic cloves
4 to 5 fresh basil leaves
$2/3$ cup chopped walnuts
$1/2$ cup good-quality olive oil
$1/2$ cup grated Parmesan cheese, plus more to garnish
$1/2$ cup grated fontina cheese
Salt and pepper to taste
1 box (16 ounces) penne pasta, cooked according to package directions, hot

Place the dandelion greens and $1^1/4$ cups of water in a medium saucepan. Bring to a boil, turn off heat, and cover for 5 minutes. The greens should be limp and very green. Uncover, drain, and let cool.

In a food processor fitted with the steel blade, chop the garlic, basil, and walnuts. Add the greens and process until finely chopped. Add the oil, grated cheeses, salt, and pepper and process to form a paste.

Toss with the freshly cooked penne pasta. Garnish with grated Parmesan cheese.

Makes 4 main-course servings

FIDDLEHEAD AU GRATIN

Fiddlehead ferns can be gathered from woodlands or purchased at a grocery store or farmstand in late May and early June. Fiddleheads are prone to carry salmonella and must be washed and boiled before using in any recipe; they should not be eaten raw.

3 cups sliced white potatoes
1 medium onion, halved
4 cups fiddlehead ferns
$1/4$ pound (1 stick) butter, melted
3 cups shredded sharp Cheddar cheese
3 tablespoons chopped fresh chives

Boil the potato slices with the onion in water to cover until just soft, 10 to 15 minutes. Drain, discard the onion, and reserve the potatoes.

Wash the fiddleheads in cold water. Place in a large stockpot with water to cover. Cook over medium-high heat until the water boils. Remove from heat and let sit for 5 to 10 minutes, until slightly tender. Drain and pat dry.

Preheat the oven to 350°F. With a pastry brush, lightly grease a 10-inch casserole dish with butter. Place a layer of $1/3$ of the potatoes in the bottom of the dish; brush with butter. Add an even layer of $1/3$ of the fiddleheads; brush with butter. Sprinkle on $1/3$ of the shredded cheese and chives. Repeat this process until all ingredients are used. Bake for 20 minutes, until the cheese is brown and bubbly.

Makes 6 servings

VIOLET AND DANDELION GREEN SALAD

Bitter greens such as dandelions are an excellent source of vitamins. Since these greens are only young and tender in the early part of spring, it is best to enjoy this salad throughout the month of May. Violets mixed with tarragon, oil, and vinegar make a simple but delicious dressing that can be used on any salad.

1 cup fresh violet blossoms
2 cups fresh violet leaves
2 cups fresh young dandelion greens
VIOLET VINEGAR DRESSING
1 cup fresh violet blossoms
1 cup white cider vinegar
2 tablespoons fresh tarragon leaves
⅓ cup olive oil
Salt and pepper

Wash all the greens well, pat dry between paper towels, and toss in a salad bowl.

TO MAKE THE violet vinegar salad dressing, In a small mixing bowl, combine all the ingredients. Cover and refrigerate for several hours before using.

Makes 4 servings

A Victorian china closet is refreshed with a coat of white paint and panels of swirled milk glass procured from a stained-glass supplier. Adopted for the bath, it becomes an elegant place to store linens and an array of handmade bath oils and waters. The key tassel for the bottom cupboard is fashioned from hemlock cones garnished with moss.

THE HOME IN SPRING It is easy to relish the gifts of the season in any room, yet the fresh scents, delicate colors, and soft textures of spring seem particularly well suited to the bath and bedroom. The healing properties of pine distilled into oils and soaps and the gentle perfume of violets infused in the bath offer an aromatherapy of tranquillity.

FOR THE BATH

Try mixing your own bath additives for a soothing touch of nature to include in your daily regime.

PINE NEEDLE BATH SALTS

Easy to make, these bath salts provide pretty hostess gifts. Add to bath water for natural scent and skin softening.

WHAT YOU'LL NEED 2 cups kosher salt • 1 to 2 clusters pine needles

1 Place an even layer of kosher salt (about 2 tablespoons) in the bottom of a glass jar. Cut 12 pine needles from the cluster and layer over the salt. Repeat, layering the salt and then the pine needles, until finished.
2 Cover tightly and let age for several weeks, until the pine scent has permeated the salts. To give as a gift, place in an attractive jar or bowl covered with parchment paper secured with twine.

PINE BATH OIL

A frequent bath additive and skin softener that looks decorative decanted into clear glass bottles.

WHAT YOU'LL NEED 2 clusters pine needles • About 2 cups baby oil, or as needed

1 Place the clusters of pine needles in a glass jar. Cover completely with the baby oil and seal the jar tightly. Age for 3 to 4 weeks, until the pine

scent has permeated the oil (see photograph on following page).
2 Strain, discard the needles, and add fresh ones to the oil.

PINE GLYCERIN SOAP

WHAT YOU'LL NEED 2 cups chopped glycerin soup (2 bars) • 2 to 3 pine clusters

1 Place the chopped glycerin soap in the top of a double boiler. Heat gently over a medium flame until fully melted. Remove frothy bubbles from the surface with a mesh skimmer and discard.
2 For molds, use either the bottom half of a quart milk carton or an aluminum soup can that has been brushed lightly with vegetable oil. Pour the melted soap into the forms, then place a pine cluster in each container of soap, or sprinkle in chopped pine needles cut with kitchen scissors. Let the soap harden for about 1 hour.
3 Remove from the molds by tearing away the paper carton or removing the bottom lid of the soup can with a can opener. Use for bathing, or wrap in cellophane tied with ribbon or twine to give as a gift.

VIOLET WATER AND GRASS WATER

Floral waters are a subtle way to fragrance a bath, make an after-bath splash, or, left in an open container, scent a room.

WHAT YOU'LL NEED 3 cups distilled water • 2 cups violet blossoms, or 2 cups grass clippings (from an untreated lawn) • 2 cups vodka • 3 drops natural violet or grass essential oil (see Natural Resources, page 123)

1 Bring the water to a boil and pour over the violet blossoms or grass clippings. Cover and let stand until fully cooled.

2 Strain the liquid, discarding the blossoms or grass, and add the vodka and essential oil. Decant into glass bottles, liquor decanters, or apothecary jars. This will last, tightly covered, for several months. Use this floral water in the bath or smooth on with a cotton ball for a refreshing skin tonic.

IN THE BEDROOM

In centuries past, herbs and flowers were dried and preserved, then stuffed into small sleep pillows to encourage sweet dreams. You can achieve the same slumber-inducing effects by simply placing a bouquet of wildflowers or a scented candle by the bed, or using sachets of pine to scent sheets, pillows, and linen closets.

PINE SACHET

Stitch up a pouch from a sheer fabric such as dotted swiss or muslin and fill with crushed pine needles. Cut up the pine needles into tiny pieces with scissors to release the fragrance (and make a softer sachet). Place in drawers, linen closets, or atop the bed to scent the bed-clothes with a woodland aroma.

SCENTED CANDLES

Candles can be purchased in a wide range of scents, but you can also add fragrance to your own candles using essential oils. You can find essential oils in aromatherapy and health food stores, or order them by mail (see Natural Resources, page 123). Choose a favorite essence— violet, spruce, grass—and use it to scent store-bought candles. Mix a 2-ounce bottle of essential oil with $\frac{1}{4}$ cup orrisroot powder (see Natural Resources, page 123) and sprinkle in the bottom of an airtight plastic storage container. Place unscented candles inside the container and store in a cool place for 4 to 6 weeks. Burn the candles to release the aroma.

Add natural accents to candles by wreathing them with blades of grass or small fern fronds, or placing them in rustic candleholders fashioned from thin birch logs. Using straight pins, affix blades of new grass to the base of a pillar candle, then tie with twine. Or place a pillar candle inside a cup, such as a silver mint julep cup, with a little water, and ring the candle with fern cuttings. To make birch candleholders, cut 2-inch-diameter birch logs into lengths of 6 to 8 inches. Drill a hole about 1 inch deep in one end using a $\frac{3}{4}$-inch bit on a drill press to create a well that will securely hold a taper candle.

PEARLY EVERLASTING

Pearly everlasting is a pleasingly fragrant wildflower that isn't fully in bloom until late summer, but it is just as captivating in spring, as it begins to bud. It is a lovely flower to place in small vases on a bedside table and to watch the blooms of slowly unfold, filling the air with a sweet aroma almost like maple syrup.

LEAFY BED LINENS

Young green oak leaves inspired this bedsheet border fashioned from leaf appliqués. Trace the new leaves onto paper to create a pattern, then pin and cut out of fabric (cream-colored silk was used here). Hand-stitch the leaves onto the top hem of the sheet, then add veining with brown thread to mimic real leaves. Leaves cut from fabric or paper can be sewn or glued onto pillows, lamp shades, curtains, and duvet covers.

A MAYFLOWER BASKET

For a contemporary update of the traditional Mayflower baskets once hung on front doors on the first of May, fashion a flower "basket" from an aluminum can. Punch two holes on opposite sides of the top rim using a tin punch or ice pick, then lace ribbon or seam binding through the holes and hang from a doorknob or bedpost. Fill with water and a cutting from a flowering tree to add a romantic breath of spring to your bedroom.

RITES OF SPRING: CELEBRATING EASTER In addition to its important religious significance, Easter is also a celebration of the rebirth of nature. Decorate eggs, symbolizing new life; gather mosses and flowers to line Easter baskets; invite family and friends for a dinner celebrating the season's bounty; and fill the house with flowering branches. Indoors and out, spring is in bloom.

AN EASY METHOD FOR HOLLOWING EGGS

WHAT YOU'LL NEED 1 dozen eggs in the carton • Straight pin • Spoon • Wooden skewer • Drinking straw • A glass

1 Leave the eggs in the carton, which will support them while keeping your hands free. Place a pin at the tip of the egg and lightly tap with the spoon (as though hammering a nail) until you've formed a hole. Insert a wooden skewer into the hole and gently press through the egg until a hole is formed in the opposite end.

2 Remove the egg from the carton and push the skewer through several times to break the yolk, making it easier to blow out. Hold the egg over a glass and place a straw over the hole. Blow through the straw until the contents of the egg have emptied into the glass. Gently wash the outer shell and let dry thoroughly before painting.

PAINTED EGGS

Instead of coloring eggs with unpredictable or garish dyes, paint them beautiful pastel hues using a flat latex-based paint and a small foam brush (available at hardware stores). Add a second coat if necessary. Painting the surface of hollow eggs strengthens the shells, so that with proper wrapping and storage, they can be reused from year to year. Nestle eggs into baskets, compotes, and urns, cushioning and accenting them with tufts of grass or moss.

A LIVING EASTER BASKET

Present Easter treats in a basket made with a living fern and moss. Simply wrap the root ball of a fern plant with sheet moss, then insert a leafy branch in one side and arch to the other side to form a handle. Fill with chocolate eggs and candies.

A GARLAND OF EGGS

String painted blown eggs together to create a garland for a doorway or window, or to use as a centerpiece for the dining table. String onto rayon or silk ribbon using a large crewel needle. Embellish the garland by tucking wildflower blossoms, violet leaves, sprigs of grass, and ferns into the openings in the eggs.

THE EASTER TABLE Delicate violets, moss-filled pots, and tiny sprouting ferns add the spirit and colors of spring to the table.

ABOVE Instead of a single centerpiece, a procession of plant pots filled with fresh grass and miniature bouquets of wild violets and ferns creates a more naturalistic tableau. Akro agate pots and a McKee jadeite pedestal echo the soft pastels of the painted eggs, all shown to advantage on a chartreuse reverse damask tablecloth from the 1930s. LEFT A bell jar fashioned from the bowl of a broken wineglass is used to coddle a new spring fern.

ABOVE The mantel echoes the table setting, with an
Art Deco urn filled with a pyramid of eggs and trimmed
with fern fronds. Pots of lavender and purple violets
and newly sprouted grass line either side. ABOVE RIGHT
Sprigs of greenery with tiny violet blossoms are tucked
beneath Bakelite silverware on linen napkins at each place.
RIGHT The elements of the centerpiece can later adorn
a sunny windowsill.

A CAKE TO CELEBRATE SPRING

This Easter confection is made from layers of
vanilla cake joined with violet-sugar syrup,
which helps keep the cake moist. The cake is
covered in a rich buttercream frosting with
intricate ferns iced in white on its sides, and a
simple bouquet of edible violets and leaves
on the top. You may use whatever white or
yellow cake recipe you like, as well as any
favorite buttercream frosting.

VIOLET SYRUP

2 cups fresh violet blossoms

3 cups boiling water

1³/₄ cups sugar

Place the violet blossoms in a small saucepan
and add the boiling water. Cover and let steep
for 2 hours.

Strain the mixture through a fine sieve or
coffee filter.

Return the liquid to the saucepan and
add the sugar. Bring to a boil, reduce heat,
and stir until thickened—about 10 minutes.
The syrup will keep, tightly covered and
refrigerated, for a month. Coat the tops of
the cake layers generously using a pastry
brush, then join together.

Violets grow in patches along the
woods and roadsides. Collect them
for tiny arrangements, or tie them
into a bouquet with ribbon for a
hostess gift or to adorn the top of
a gift box.

The world is at its most LUSH now, brimming with WILDFLOWERS, meadow GRASSES, and hedges of plump BERRIES. Gracefully arching trees create a CANOPY OF GREEN to shelter outdoor tables and dapple hammocks with sunlight. SEA-SHELLS and WAVE-SMOOTHED STONES gathered on BEACH WALKS accumulate on tables and windowsills. The GARDEN is an ever-changing panoply of color and texture, overflowing with its BOUNTY. At night, the PERFUME OF FLOWERS or salt spray from the ocean scents the air, while the blinking signals of LIGHTNING BUGS form a staccato syncopation against the steady rhythm of CRICKETS. Set a table outside, pour a tall glass of LEMONADE spiked with fresh mint or a Raspberry Cooler, and watch the summer sun set. This is a season not to be rushed.

THE NATURAL GARDEN The wooded forests and open meadows of the countryside are filled with inspiration for garden plans and plantings. I've always marveled at the unstudied beauty of fallen trees in the woods, with patches of moss creeping over their trunks and feathery ferns poking up around them, or the breathtaking sight of a whole meadow colored in a kaleidoscope of daisies and lupine and Indian paintbrush. I love the subtler splendor of wild grasses as well, textured with spiky plumes and distinctive seedpods. Today, gardeners are introducing a more natural look to flower beds and lawns, using native grasses, ferns, and wildflowers in place of care-intensive flowers, lawns, and shrubs. Grass and wildflower seeds are available through seed catalogs or can be gathered from the wild, and seeds and plants may be purchased at garden centers (see Wildflowers for Gardens, page 117). The plan of the garden can be more relaxed as well, designed to allow nature to have free rein. You can introduce rocks and ledges as natural pathways that moss and lichen can thrive on. Trellises can be crafted from fallen trees to form a base for creeping vines such as bittersweet and roses, while tender twigs can be used to train ivy and myrtle topiaries.

GARDEN PATHS

Paths carved through the garden provide a perspective from which to observe and enjoy the flowers and plants that grow there. Create a natural walkway with stones culled from the beach, or fallen trees cut into half-round logs.

Garden steps are created with found slabs of granite and stone. A stone-terraced ledge can become a functioning garden, with soil added between the rocks and planted with grasses, herbs, and perennials. The more elaborate rock-ledge path at right is naturally overgrown with ferns and wild violets.

Large white stones gathered from the beach, below, form a mosaic path through a patch of grasses and ferns. Dig shallow holes for the stones, then firmly press them into the dirt. Scallop shells, round slices of logs, or pieces of slate could also be used to create walkways.

TWIG TRELLISES

A natural trellis, left, is constructed from black locust tree limbs and supple young branches bent into arches. The slats of the trellis provide a structure for climbing roses and morning glories to creep over, and will eventually create a shaded walkway.

Twig trellises can be made on a smaller scale for training ivy plants into cone-shaped topiaries, above. And moss gathered from the woods can be placed around the base of potted plants and herbs to help keep them from drying out.

SUMMER FLOWERS You don't need a green thumb or even a garden to fill your house with glorious summer flowers. Grab a pail of water and a sharp pair of cutting shears, and head out for a walk along a roadside or meadow to gather wildflowers. Keep these guidelines in mind:

1 Do not cut wildflowers from protected lands, and make sure the wildflowers you do pick are not endangered (see Wildflowers for Cutting, page 116).

2 Pick flowers early in the morning before the heat of the summer sun saps their moisture and strength.

3 Make select cuttings, always leaving some flowers and seeds on each plant, so that it can reseed itself.

Tips for Keeping Cut Flowers Fresh

1 Clean the gathering pail with bleach and hot water. Fill with lukewarm water.

2 Place freshly cut wildflowers directly into water.

3 Let the flowers stand in water, drinking up moisture, for several hours before arranging.

4 Clean the vase or container you'll be using with bleach and hot water.

5 Fill the vase with a mixture of 1 tablespoon of sugar to 1 gallon of water.

6 Add an aspirin tablet to the water and let dissolve.

7 Arrange the flowers in the vase, recutting stems on an angle so they have more surface area to drink up water.

DAISIES

Daisies are one of the most familiar of all wildflowers. In early summer, whole stands of them bloom in meadows and on roadsides. A field of daisies reappears year after year in the same place because the flowers continually reseed themselves. But the daisy's ubiquity doesn't lessen its endearing simplicity. What child (or adult) hasn't plucked its petals, secretly chanting, "He loves me, he loves me not"? I remember childhood afternoons spent picking daisies with my sister, who braided them into bracelets and hairbands. I always watched with fascination as she intertwined the stems to create a chain of flowers. Daisy garlands can be used to swag tables and doorways, as well as to crown a child's head.

HOW TO MAKE A DAISY GARLAND

Cut 12 to 15 daisies, leaving stems 10 to 12 inches long. Begin by placing 3 blossoms on a flat surface at varied heights and braid the stems together once. Then add a fourth daisy to the center of the flowers and braid into the chain. Continue braiding until all the flowers are woven in. Tie off the stem end with seam binding. To make longer garlands, join braided sections together with florist's wire.

LUPINE

In mountainous regions of the country, vast fields are carpeted in colorful lupines. Lupine is a self-seeding, spiky blossom, similar to delphinium, that blooms in shades of blue, purple, pink, and white. In Sugar Hill, New Hampshire, the lupine fields are so breathtakingly beautiful, this tiny town has created an annual festival in early June to celebrate the arrival of the lupine. Once the flowers' blooms have faded, their seedpods dry on the stalk, then crack open to reseed the ground.

FRAMING FERNS AND LEAVES

Once dried, leaves and ferns are best framed simply—between two sheets of glass joined with bookbinding tape—which won't compete for attention with the shapely graphic silhouettes of the leaves. (Artists' acrylic clear coat spray, bulldog clips, and linen bookbinding tape are available at office supply, crafts, or art stores, or see Natural Resources, page 123. White gloves, which reduce the potential for smudging the glass, are available at photo supply and camera shops.)

WHAT YOU'LL NEED Pressed and fully dried leaf or fern frond • Artists' acrylic clear coat spray • 2 sheets clear glass, cut to the same dimensions • Window cleaner and newspaper • White gloves • Bulldog clips • Linen bookbinding tape

1 Spray each side of the leaf or fern with a coat of artists' clear acrylic spray and let fully dry. This will help protect the color of the foliage.
2 Thoroughly clean both sides of the glass with window cleaner and newspaper.
3 Wearing gloves, place the fern or leaf in the center of the glass in the desired position. Place the second piece of glass on top.

4 Clamp the 2 long sides with bulldog clips to hold the glass in place while you tape the top and bottom edges. Cut the tape to the correct length, center over each end, and smoothly adhere. Move the clips to the top and bottom edges, and tape the sides.
5 Display on a shelf or easel away from direct sunlight.

OUTDOOR ENTERTAINING Part of the liberation of summer is transplanting activities that are typically confined indoors into the freedom of the outdoors. A simple meal becomes a special occasion when it's set under the stars or enjoyed as a picnic by the sea. We tend to take an overly casual approach to outdoor dining, using paper plates, plastic forks and knives, and disposable cups. Not only is this environmentally unfriendly, it also isn't the prettiest way to savor a meal alfresco. For a real treat, why not move a small table outside, set it with your best china and crystal, and create a sumptuous dining experience beneath the trees?

A pale lavender linen tablecloth draped over a round table is weighted with white stones gathered from the beach to protect the setting from a gusty breeze. Antique glass bottles are filled with simple meadow grasses. Napkins folded into triangles to encase vintage silverware are beribboned with a blade of wild grass, with feathery plumes of timothy grass tucked inside.

Use natural elements such as leaves and fern fronds to enhance a simple tabletop. ABOVE LEFT A freshly cut fern is sandwiched between a white ironstone charger and a translucent amber plate for an eye-catching place setting. LEFT A large ironstone platter is framed by a fan of fern bracts placed beneath it to dramatic effect. Glass serving pieces rest on a bed of green oak leaves. ABOVE A glass martini shaker filled with lemonade and set into a silver coaster edged with wild grass is the picture of summer ease.

NATURAL BERRIES

Summer is filled with an abundance of fresh fruits and vegetables, but there is nothing quite like the sweetly ripe, melt-in-your-mouth juiciness of wild berries. Store-bought berries are no match for what you can find (for free) in the wild. From June through August, there is a succession of delicious berries to choose from—strawberries, blackberries, raspberries, huckleberries, blueberries —to just pop into your mouth, sprinkle over freshly whipped cream, or bake into pies.

Preparing Summer Berries

1 Make sure you have identified wild berries as safe in a guidebook before gathering or eating them.

2 Make sure the berries are ready for picking—they should be soft and ripe, not at all green, but also not starting to overripen and rot.

3 Place gathered berries on a flat surface such as a tray, baking sheet, or shallow basket in a single layer. If you fill a whole pail with berries, the ones at the bottom will most likely be crushed.

4 Gently spray the berries with water to clean them just before they are eaten or used in a recipe. High water pressure can bruise fragile berries.

5 Most summer berries should be used immediately, though blueberries will keep for a week in the refrigerator.

Wild strawberry plants produce tiny white blossoms that turn into miniature red berries. These, like most wild berries, are small in size but big in flavor.

BLUEBERRY SCALLION VINEGAR

Summer salads take on a surprising twist with a sprinkling of blueberries or ripe red raspberries. Make a berry vinegar to add the flavor of summer to salads any time of the year—try this one in a vinaigrette to dress a mixture of red lettuce and slivered almonds.

>   45 to 50 blueberries
>   5 to 6 scallions (green onions)
>   About 3 cups white wine vinegar,
>   or as needed

Mash 30 of the blueberries, strain, and place the juices in a glass bottle (old wine bottles work well). Add 3 whole scallion stalks and fill with white vinegar. Cork tightly and place in a sunny window for several weeks.

Once the vinegar has aged, strain it and decant into a pretty bottle or apothecary jar, adding 2 or 3 fresh scallions and 15 to 20 whole blueberries.

To give as a gift, dip the tightly corked top of the bottle into melted wax and tie on a bar pourer (a metal spout atop a cork) with a piece of ribbon or twine.

Makes 3^1/$_2$ to 4 cups

RASPBERRY COOLER

>   Fresh Berry Syrup (recipe follows)
>   4 liters seltzer water
>   4 cups chopped ice
>   Fresh raspberries for garnish

Pour cooled Fresh Berry Syrup into the bottom of a punch bowl or large pitcher. Stir in the seltzer water. Add ice and garnish with fresh raspberries.

Makes 12 servings

FRESH BERRY SYRUP

A sauce made from freshly picked raspberries and blackberries can be used as a syrup for pancakes, or as a dessert sauce for vanilla ice cream or airy angel food cake. Or try diluting it with seltzer water and adding a few fresh berries for a refreshing summer drink.

>   2 cups fresh raspberries or blackberries
>   3 cups sugar

Mash the berries into a pulp. Add the sugar, then heat in a medium saucepan over low heat until the sugar has dissolved and the mixture thickens, about 5 minutes. Store in an airtight jar in the refrigerator for up to 1 week.

Makes 8 servings

RASPBERRY AND BLACKBERRY CHICKEN

Berries aren't just for dessert: they can also enhance a main course, such as these chicken breasts with fresh berries slipped under the skin.

2 whole chicken breasts, split
Salt and pepper to taste
2 cups mixed fresh blackberries and raspberries
6 scallions (green onions), chopped
2 tablespoons chopped chives
1 tablespoon olive oil
1 medium onion, sliced

Rinse and pat dry the chicken breasts, leaving the skin on. Loosen the chicken skin from the breast meat to create a pocket. Lightly salt and pepper the surface of the breast.

In a small bowl, place 1 cup of the mixed berries and mash with a fork until juice forms. Add the chopped scallions and chives and blend. Pour over the meat and marinate, covered, in the refrigerator for several hours.

Preheat the oven to 350°F. Place the chicken in an 8 × 8-inch baking dish greased with olive oil (discarding the marinade). Stuff ¼ of the sliced onion and ¼ cup of the berries beneath the skin of each chicken breast. Bake for 45 to 50 minutes, until the juices run clear when the meat is cut with a knife.

Makes 4 servings

STRAWBERRY CREAM PUFFS

Berries are wonderfully suited to accompany summer desserts such as pastries and fruit compotes. A fluff of brandied whipped cream and a sprinkle of berries make a delicious dessert on their own, or you can use them as filling for a baked pastry puff.

> 2 cups wild strawberries
> 1 package frozen puff pastry
> 8 ounces whipping cream, ice-cold
> 1 tablespoon sugar
> 1 teaspoon brandy
> Medium-size metal bowl and beaters from a handheld mixer, or a whisk, all chilled for 30 minutes in the refrigerator

Gently wash the berries and dry on a cookie sheet lined with paper towels.

Bake pastries according to package instructions. Cool on a wire rack and then split each pastry in half.

Place the whipping cream, sugar, and brandy in the chilled mixing bowl and mix on medium speed or whisk until soft peaks form.

Place one half of each of the pastries on its serving plate. Fill with 1/4 of the brandied cream and 1/2 cup strawberries, then top with the remaining half of the pastry and a dollop of the remaining whipped cream. Garnish with remaining berries and their leaves and serve immediately.

Makes 4 servings

SENSORY PLEASURES: SUMMER SOUNDS

Whether you are out in the garden, walking in the woods, or sleeping by an open window, there are many wonderful sounds in summer that we often tune out or take for granted. Start listening more closely to the melodies that warm weather and wide-open windows invite into your home— they may even lull you to sleep.

- Bumblebees buzzing on a blossom

- Birdsong

- The gentle percussion of rain on the roof

- The rumble of approaching thunder gradually intensifying into chilling claps and crackles

- The soft rustle of leaves in the breeze

- The rushing or trickling babble of a brook or stream; the quiet lapping of a lake against the shore

- The steady rhythm of the ocean waves tumbling, or their soft roar replicated inside a conch shell

- The loud hum of crickets and cicadas

THE HOME IN SUMMER Whether you have the luxury of living near a beach, or just the occasional pleasure of visiting one, you are likely to find yourself strolling the shore and stopping to gather shells and stones. It seems almost instinctual to gravitate toward the teeming life by the shore—as children we are fascinated by seashells and sea glass, crabs and starfish. It's no wonder we always return home with sand in our pockets.

GATHERING SEASHELLS

Seashells can be collected most easily in wire or mesh baskets. The baskets are light, allowing a large quantity of stones and shells to be gathered, and they can be placed under a faucet or garden hose for easy cleaning. Dry cleaned shells on a flat window screen or sheet of framed chicken wire in a sunny spot with good circulation to eliminate any strong seaside odors.

OPPOSITE Bleached starfish make a summery collage tacked to the wall (with sparing amounts of hot glue). Bleach starfish in a solution of 1 quart water to 1 cup bleach. Soak for 30 minutes, then lay them in the sun for 3 hours. When dry, they will have a white chalky finish.

OPPOSITE A rolling glass-topped table has a modern seaside motif: its two layers of glass become a display case for starfish and sand dollars. Place the first sheet of glass, cut to size, on the tabletop, then affix to it 4 acrylic cubes (available at crafts stores) with epoxy glue. Arrange starfish and shells as desired. Apply epoxy to the tops of the cubes, then adhere the top piece of glass.

THIS PAGE Seashells add graphic interest to a room pared down for minimalist summer living. The sun-bleached lineup on the mantel boasts the bounty of beach foraging: ocean-smoothed stones, the whorl of a conch shell, an assortment of starfish. On the side table, an antique garden cloche in pale lavender that was once used to force ferns now shows off prized beach finds. The table is garnished with a clever drawer pull—a simple, sturdy scallop shell. Attach a hex nut to the inside of a shell with epoxy glue. Let dry, then screw onto drawer front.

SEA GLASS THAT SHINES

Opposite, one of the many coast-line collectibles treasured by beachcombers is sea glass, small shards of man-made glass that have been tumbled smooth, transformed by the churning tide. Many people display these frosted blue, green, clear, and amber pieces of glass in bowls or jars on windowsills to catch the sunlight, but you can also show them off in an illuminated jar that has been wired as a lamp. Find a nicely shaped clear glass jar or vase, and have a hole drilled in its side at a hardware store or glass cutter's. Then have the lamp wired like a small night light, using a short candle-base socket and pilot or night-light bulb. Fill with sea glass (be sure to cover the bulb and hardware) for a magical night light.

STONE MOSAIC FRAME

Stones collected from the beach or river can be used to form a naturalistic mosaic on a picture frame or mirror.

WHAT YOU'LL NEED 30 to 40 small white beach stones • 2-inch-wide wood frame • Epoxy • 12-ounce container of ready-mixed plaster

1 Wash stones under cold water to remove sand and soil, and let dry.
2 Place the frame flat on a work surface. Arrange the stones on the frame in desired pattern.
3 Cover the back of each stone with epoxy and affix it to the frame. Let the epoxy dry for 8 to 12 hours, until the stones are firmly adhered.

4 Grout between the stones with ready-mixed plaster, using a damp rag to remove excess plaster from stone surfaces. Let the plaster dry for 1 to 2 days, until firm. Then clean off any remaining dried plaster on the stones using warm water and steel wool. Fit the frame with glass and a favorite picture or a piece of mirror.

Autumn

The hint of a CHILL tinges the air in early morning and evening, reinvigorating us and presaging the spectacular TRANSFORMATION about to unfold. TREES will soon be painted in CRIMSON, ORANGE, and GOLD, flaming across the hillside like a vibrant fire. The HARVEST begins, as cranberries ripen in the bogs and wild grapes grow heavy on the vine. It is a season of DRAMA, and we have an almost primal need to immerse ourselves in it, since the brilliant PAGEANT will last but a few weeks. Savor autumn's beauty by GATHERING and preserving leaves and berries to adorn your home and cooking flavorful meals with tart CRANBERRIES and rich chest-nuts. Grab a SWEATER and head out into a CRISP autumn afternoon to enjoy the last of the sun's warmth and a front-row seat for the FOLIAGE'S showstopping finale.

LEAVES OF GOLD As the last of the flowers begin to fade, it is the hues of autumn leaves that fill the landscape. This transformation occurs as the days grow shorter and there is less light for leaves to produce the chlorophyll that keeps them green. So the skyline undergoes a continuing evolution—sugar maples turn brilliant shades, from marigold to pumpkin to red; birch trees take on a golden glow; and oak trees adopt a sophisticated palette ranging from copper to burgundy. Preserve and extend the beauty of these leaves with the following projects and ideas.

CHANGING COLORS

Observe the metamorphosis of color up close by bringing leafy branches indoors just as they begin to change. Once the process has started, it will continue—even indoors—until the leaves have fallen from the branch. Cut branches will last for up to a week.

1 Cut the branch just above the nub where another branch will start or already exists.

2 Smash the stems of the branch with a hammer and place into tepid water for 10 minutes.

3 Add cool water and let stand for several hours before arranging in a large vase or flower bucket.

PRESSED LEAVES

Autumn leaves can be preserved at their peak by drying and pressing, and then used for projects such as decoupage and framing. Use a flower press (see page 68) or simply place each leaf between separate pages of a book or encyclopedia, then weight with a brick or heavy rock. In 7 to 10 days, the leaves will be flat and dry.

SENSORY PLEASURES: AUTUMN SIGHTS

There is much to dazzle the eye in fall—take time to stop and savor all the visual wonders:

- The mural of deciduous trees against a bright azure sky and a Persian carpet of multicolored leaves underfoot.

- The early-morning mist hanging softly in the air; a dusting of sparkling frost blanketing the ground like diamonds

- Overhead, birds beginning their migration— flocks of robins and wild geese soaring in V-shaped formations

- Even the path of the wind is visible, as trees bend in the breeze and leaves take flight like kites on a string

- Fields and meadows glimmering with goldenrod and roadsides edged with fluffy white blossoms of pearly everlasting

- The evening sky filled with shimmering starlight and the glow of a harvest moon

OPPOSITE Maple and oak leaves make a dramatic arrangement in yellow and chartreuse pottery from the 1940s.

HOW TO MAKE A FLOWER PRESS

Flower presses are available at art stores and through gardening catalogs, but it is also fairly easy to make your own.

WHAT YOU'LL NEED Drill with $\frac{1}{4}$-inch bit • 2 pieces of $\frac{1}{2}$-inch plywood cut to 14 × 14 inches • 2 yards birch tape • 50 sheets of unprinted newsprint cut to 14 × 14 inches • 10 sheets of mat board precut to 14 × 14 inches by a framing studio • 4 (4-inch) flathead screws with wing nuts

1 Using the $\frac{1}{4}$-inch drill bit, drill a hole approximately 1 inch in from each corner of each piece of plywood (8 holes total for 2 pieces of wood).
2 Cut the birch tape to the length of each side of the wood and adhere it to the unfinished edges using a hot iron.
3 Measuring in 1 inch from each corner of paper and mat board, cut off the corners on the diagonal, in order to allow room for the screws.
4 Place stacks of 10 sheets of paper between each layer of mat board.
5 Press leaves or ferns between the paper sheets. Then bookend with the pieces of plywood. Insert the screws into the holes and screw on the wing nuts as tightly as possible. Leaves will be pressed and dried in 10 days to 2 weeks.

GLYCERIN-PRESERVED LEAVES

Leaves dried with glycerin have a soft, supple texture that is long-lasting. This is a good method for leaves that will be used in wreaths, swags, and garlands. Leaves dried in glycerin turn a much darker hue, so it is best to start with brightly colored yellow and orange leaves. (This process is less effective in humid areas, in which glycerin-treated leaves tend to "weep" and discolor.)

WHAT YOU'LL NEED Bucket • 1 gallon of water • 4 cups glycerin (available at a pharmacy, or see Natural Resources, page 123) • 8 to 10 cut branches of leaves (see Note, below) • Hammer

1 Fill a bucket with the gallon of water and mix in the glycerin.
2 Smash the stems of the branches with a hammer and place in the bucket. Keep in a dry, dark place for 3 to 5 days, until the branches have thoroughly soaked up the water-glycerin mixture.
3 You can use the branches as they are or use just the leaves.
NOTE Using pruning shears or clippers, cut branches at their peak of color—before there is a frost and too many leaves have already fallen from the tree.

TO MAKE A WINDOW SWAG
Start with 1½ yards of armature wire for the base. Using green florists' wire, attach clusters of 5 to 7 glycerin-preserved leaves to the wire base. Suspend the swag from cup hooks on each side at the top of a window frame.

COLOR-COPIED LEAVES

Color photocopies of leaves look surprisingly lifelike and make great motifs for decoupage projects, such as wooden boxes or tabletops, or for framing—the "leaves" will never become dry, brittle, or discolored (see The Most Colorful Autumn Leaves, page 118). Select an assortment of brilliantly colored leaves, from green to scarlet, and place them directly onto a color photocopier (fit as many as you can on a page). Cut out and use to create a wall border, cover a lamp shade, or decoupage to the front of a journal or photo album.

OPPOSITE To dazzle a wall with a dash of autumn: affix a sprinkling of color-copied leaves using removable adhesive; use a foam roller to smooth away any bubbles. LEFT A selection of pressed maple and oak leaves becomes a work of art mounted on mat board and framed in an antique six-panel frame. For best results and to reduce fading, spray leaves with a coat of clear acrylic (available at art or hardware stores, or see Natural Resources, page 123) before framing, or use color-copied leaves. BELOW Color-copied maple leaves are scattered across a flea-market tabletop as if by an autumn breeze. Cut out paper leaves, position in place, then top with a piece of clear glass cut to the size of the tabletop.

CLOCKWISE FROM TOP LEFT

SUMAC BERRIES These festive red plumes are best if collected after a heavy frost, once the sumac's leaves have fallen and plunging temperatures have turned the berries a brilliant burgundy. BITTERSWEET Collect bittersweet berries while their outer casings are still green. Hang in a dry place overnight and the shells will pop open to reveal vibrant orange berries with bright yellow petals. Cold temperatures tend to soften the berries, so collect before a heavy frost. CHRISTMAS HOLLY BERRIES These bright red berries grow on the outskirts of damp marsh and bog areas. Their long-lasting color makes them a good choice for wreaths and window boxes. Pick after a frost, when they have shed most of their leaves. HIGH BUSH CRANBERRIES These bright and translucent red berries grow in bunches on bushes similar to high-bush blueberries. Pick berries before a frost when they are firm and colorful. Once berries have passed, place on a tree for birds to eat.

BOUNTIFUL BERRIES Autumn is an ideal time to gather berries for making wreaths, arrangements, or window boxes. The woods, marshes, and fields are filled with a multitude of ripe, colorful berries, from rose hips in reddish orange to deep red hawthorn. Fill baskets with berries for a welcoming flourish outside on the porch, or hang on the door a swag of berried branches tied together with ribbon. A window box of fading flowers can be rejuvenated for fall with berries, pods, and dried leaves.

LEFT A colorful wreath of autumn leaves and berries strikes a seasonal note hung on a mirror or above a mantel. Using green florists' wire, attach bitter-sweet, high-bush cranberries, and maple leaves to an 8-inch wire wreath form. Hung outside in an area protected from the rain, the wreath will last well into the holiday season. BELOW Colorful maple leaves, sumac berries, and bitter-sweet branches fill an aluminum window box fashioned from a bakery loaf pan. Spray aluminum pans with acrylic sealant to protect from rust and discoloration. Fill with sand and stones, then arrange leaves and berries as desired, anchoring their stems in the stones.

AUTUMN ENTERTAINING Take advantage of the chance to enjoy the last crisp, sun-warmed afternoons with a picnic outing beside a lake or stream or just in your own backyard. Pack up wicker baskets and a folding table, along with an array of casual foods that are easy to savor *en plein air.*

OPPOSITE The table is dressed in shades of autumn. Russell Wright plates from the 1960s, hand-blown amethyst glasses, and bamboo and Bakelite flatware from the 1940s form a rich mix of colors and textures. Tiny purple asters, the last flowers to bloom before snow arrives, are cut into tiny clusters and tucked into the fold of each napkin. Rather than a single centerpiece, there is a multicultural assortment of containers running down the center of the table, from an Art Deco vase and a hand-carved wooden bowl to a French ivory cup and an old yellowware bottle. Invite picnic guests to forage for flowers and foliage to fill the containers with bittersweet berries, golden leaves, wild grasses, and flower pods. Cranberries and wild grapes are heaped into the wooden bowl in the center. A scattering of leaves collected from the ground adds sunny color and an informal ambiance to the table.

CHESTNUT SOUP

Chestnuts grow in clusters of prickly pods. In order to avoid eating horse chestnuts, which are poisonous, it is important to identify in a guidebook the type of chestnut you are foraging. Let the pods dry in a warm, dry place until they crack open. Then remove the chestnuts.

  2 pounds fresh chestnuts
  2¾ cups milk
  1½ cups dehydrated porcini mushrooms
  ½ cup butter, melted
  1 medium onion, finely chopped
  2 garlic cloves, minced
  ½ cup all-purpose flour
  2 cups chicken stock
  2 cups cream
  1 cup vermouth
  Salt and pepper to taste
  ¼ cup chopped scallions (green onions),
    for garnish

Wash the chestnuts in cold water, then soak in lukewarm water for 20 to 25 minutes to soften the shells. Using a sharp paring knife, score the rounded side of each chestnut with a shallow *x*.

In a medium saucepan, cover the chestnuts amply with water; cover and bring to a boil over high heat; boil for 25 minutes. Scoop the chestnuts out of the water a few at a time and peel them while still very warm (remove both the outer shell and the wrinkled inner skin). Place the chestnuts in a clean saucepan and cover with the milk. Simmer over medium heat until they absorb all the milk.

In the meantime, place the mushrooms in 3 cups of water and let them stand for 2 hours. Then drain, fill with 3 more cups of water, let

stand another 2 hours, and drain again.

Just before the mushrooms have finished soaking, start the cream sauce base. In a stockpot over medium heat, melt the butter, then sauté the onion and garlic until tender, about 5 minutes. Reduce heat to low and stir in the flour until smooth. Add the chicken stock, cream, vermouth, salt, and pepper. Cook over medium heat until thickened, about 5 minutes, stirring frequently. Place the chestnuts in a food processor fitted with the steel blade. Add the mushrooms and half the soup base and puree until smooth. Fold the puree into the remaining soup. Serve warm with a garnish of chopped scallions.

Makes six 1-cup servings

THE CRUNCH OF FRESH CRANBERRIES

Cranberries have a delicious sharp, sweet-and-sour flavor that adds punch to a diversity of dishes — cakes and breads, relishes, preserves, and even tea. It is best to purchase these berries from commercial growers, leaving the cranberries growing in bogs for the wildlife that depend on them.

CRANBERRY RELISH

Mix chopped cranberries with wild grapes, walnuts, and raspberries to create a fruity relish to sandwich between freshly baked sugar cookies. Wild grapes can be found creeping over stone walls and around tree trunks and cascading over rock ledges. It's best to forage for them in late fall, when they are deep purple and the fruit has been sweetened by a frost.

This fruit-and-cookie sandwich is great to pack for picnics. Or, warm and serve with vanilla ice cream for a more sophisticated presentation.

ABOVE Relish-filled sugar cookies are a tasty and easy-to-assemble dessert for an autumn outing. OPPOSITE The soup is served in a collection of covered compotes and Asian rice bowls in shades of orange and yellow.

> 2 cups freshly chopped cranberries
> 1 cup chopped wild grapes
> 3/4 cup chopped walnuts
> 1 cup mashed raspberries
> 3/4 cup raspberry preserves

Chop and mix all the ingredients 1 day before serving to allow the flavors to blend. The relish keeps for at least 1 week tightly covered in the refrigerator.

Makes 5 cups

CRANBERRY COUSCOUS STUFFING

Cranberries and couscous create a light, piquant alternative to traditional bread stuffing. Use to stuff a turkey, chicken, or game bird, or serve as a side dish.

2 tablespoons garlic-flavored olive oil
3 garlic cloves, minced
3/4 cup yellow onion, finely chopped
2 1/2 cups chicken broth with
    fat skimmed off
1 1/2 cups couscous
3/4 cup chopped cranberries
1/3 cup honey
Salt and pepper, if desired

In a saucepan over medium heat, combine the olive oil, garlic, and onion and sauté until tender, about 5 minutes. Add the chicken broth and bring to a full boil. Add the couscous, cranberries, and honey and stir until mixed. Remove from heat and cover until the couscous has absorbed all of the liquid. Fluff with a fork, add salt and pepper to taste, and serve.

Makes 4 servings

WILD GRAPE AND CRANBERRY COBBLER

This cobbler is simply a less fussy form of a pastry-crust pie.

FILLING
3 cups halved seedless grapes
3 cups halved cranberries
3/4 cup sugar
2 tablespoons all-purpose flour
2 tablespoons orange juice
Dash of cinnamon
Dash of nutmeg
PIE CRUST
2 1/2 cups all-purpose flour
1 teaspoon salt
1 1/2 teaspoons sugar
1 cup (2 sticks) unsalted butter, chilled
    and cut into pieces
1/4 cup ice water
Vanilla ice cream, for serving (optional)

Preheat the oven to 400° F.

To make the filling, mix all the filling ingredients together and set aside.

To make the pie crust, in a food processor, mix the flour, salt, and sugar. Slowly add the butter to the mixture and mix until the dough begins to stick together. Slowly add ice water until a ball begins to form. Place it in a bowl, cover, and refrigerate for 1 hour. Roll it out on a floured surface until it is 18 inches in diameter. Center it in a 9-inch deep-dish pie plate. Fill with the fruit mixture, then fold the remaining dough over the filling.

Bake for 50 to 60 minutes, until juices begin to bubble. Remove from the oven and cool on a wire rack for 20 minutes. Serve warm with vanilla ice cream, if desired.

Makes 6 servings

LEFT A deep-dish yellowware pie plate allows this cobbler to be filled plentifully with the fruits of the season. BELOW A cozy cup of cranberry tea is served up in a Russell Wright tea cup.

SPICY CRANBERRY TEA

This tart, fragrant tea takes the chill off a brisk autumn day. Fill a Thermos or a teapot and savor its warmth and aroma.

 4 cups spring water
 4 cups cranberry juice
 4 orange pekoe tea bags
 $3/4$ teaspoon cinnamon
 1 tablespoon sugar
 16 cloves
 1 Macintosh apple, cut into 8 slices, with seeds removed
 16 whole fresh cranberries for garnish (optional)

In a saucepan over medium heat, combine the water and juice and bring to a boil.

Place the tea bags in boiling water and cranberry juice mixture, remove from heat, and let steep for 10 minutes. Remove the tea bags and add the cinnamon and sugar, stirring until the sugar dissolves.

Place 2 cloves in each apple slice and add to the tea. Cover and let steep for 5 more minutes. Pour into warmed tea cups or mugs and garnish with the apple slices and cranberries.

Makes 8 cups

LEFT The paint color for this room was chosen by matching pieces of bark from a maple tree to a paint chip. The base pigment of this shade is a greenish hue (the base is usually the bottom color on a strip of paint chips), which complements the seasonal greens regularly on display in this room. Arts and Crafts furniture has a modern appeal covered in solid linens and cottons the color of woodland greens. Potted grass and autumn's last green leaves fill a collection of soft green Art Deco pottery. A pinecone rosette makes a natural button stitched onto a linen pillow. BELOW A collection of baskets stores wool throws, pillows, and birch logs. Baskets are lined with a natural moth chaser of cedar and pine. To make, mix 4 cups cedar chips, 4 cups cut pine needles, and 3 cups tiny hemlock cones. To use in drawers and closets, place in sachet bags; for lining the bottom of a storage basket or chest, cover with a piece of fabric.

THE HOME IN AUTUMN As the days shorten, we, like the animals, turn our attention to our nests. It is a wonderful time to bring nature into the home, to foster a sense of connection, instead of isolation, as we start to spend more time indoors. Slip preserved autumn leaves beneath a glass-topped table, make a terrarium of woodland plants, create natural moth chasers with cedar and pine, and transplant wild grasses indoors as a reminder of fall's beauty as it starts to fade away.

LEFT The silhouette of a hay-scented fern adds elegant interest to a simple white lamp shade. Press and dry the fern (see page 47). Then, using white glue thinned with water and an artist's paintbrush, lightly glue the back of the fern and position it on the shade. Hold in place with small bulldog clips until dry. BELOW The missing pull chain for this lamp was replaced by braided twine and a tiny pinecone.

IN THE LIVING ROOM

Not only can you incorporate elements from nature into accessories for your home, nature can also be mined in subtler ways, letting it inspire your choice of materials and color palette. From the gray-green of lichen to the verdant hues of woodland moss, from the creamy white of Queen Anne's lace to the taupe of maple bark, hues drawn from nature can be used as the basis for wall or ceiling color choices or can be picked up in fabrics and furnishings. It is easier to decorate with natural materials such as cotton and linen fabrics, wooden furniture, and stone floors, because nature's textures and colors always harmonize well, in subtle and soothing ways that don't require much fuss and are likely to stand the test of time.

NATURAL TERRARIUMS

You may remember making terrariums as a child, but they are still an interesting way to preserve woodland plants in a self-sustaining environment. You will need a glass dome and plate, a fishbowl with a lid, or a covered jar. Collect a mixture of ferns, grasses, and moss—here, we've used sheet moss, ferns, grass, partridge berries, silver lichen, and British soldiers. Cover the bottom of the container with stones for drainage, then top with a thin layer of soil. Nestle the plants you've collected in the soil and cover with sheet moss. Cover the terrarium. Place in a partly sunny area and watch your natural garden thrive. No watering is necessary—the moisture from the plants provides its own rehydration. Remove the cover every two weeks for about an hour to prevent mold.

OPPOSITE An assortment of improvised terrariums has been fashioned from alabaster and pottery compotes and vases topped with clear glass cheese domes and a clock case. Grasses, mosses, ferns, and even tiny trees thrive in these self-contained microsystems.

The world appears to be almost FROZEN in time in winter, with bare-branched trees carving elegant SILHOUETTES against the GRAY SKY, ponds stilled by shimmering ICE, and the frigid chill suspending even our breath in the air. In the sometimes seemingly bleak landscape of winter, SNOW offers redemption. Its infinitely varied CRYSTALS fall through the sky, slowly accumulating to transform every surface with a coating of WHITE. No matter what our age, we become children again, lured outside by the downy DRIFTS. Long before Christmas was celebrated, pagan and Druid cultures honored the winter SOLSTICE by bringing greenery inside as a reminder that the earth's BOUNTY would return. You can extend an appreciation of nature by making evergreens, berries, and PINECONES part of your decor all winter long.

EVERGREENS The astringent, fresh scent of evergreen is used in aromatherapy as a soothing antidepressant. It's no wonder, then, that in the darkness of winter we bring fir trees and pine boughs inside to fill the air with this enchanting aroma. In addition to the traditional Christmas tree, add the fragrance of evergreen with wreaths, a bouquet of cut greens, or natural essential oils mixed into potpourri or placed on a lightbulb to scent a room.

COLLECTING CONES

Many different kinds of evergreens produce and drop their seed cones at the end of autumn, creating a varied tapestry of shapes and sizes that can be easily gathered for ornaments, potpourris, and decorations. (For a listing, see Pinecones, page 128.) Early winter is a good time to collect them, after the autumn leaves have blown away, and before the snow has fallen. Woven baskets are good for collecting cones—they are lightweight but roomy. If cones are damp or not fully opened, place them on a flat screen in a warm, dry place for five days to a week.

CHOOSING A CHRISTMAS TREE

The best Christmas tree is a living tree that is either potted or has its roots balled and wrapped in burlap. These trees can be brought inside for the holidays and then replanted outdoors. Acclimatize them to indoor temperatures by first storing them in an unheated garage or basement for several days. Keep indoors for no more than a week, then repeat the acclimatizing process before planting outside. It is best to dig a hole to replant the tree before a deep frost sets in, so the ground won't be too frozen for planting.

Outfit a sled with baskets and florists' or sap buckets to collect evergreens, pinecones, twigs, and sumac berries after a heavy snow. Not only are these natural elements easier to see after a snowstorm, when they are thrown into relief against the white, children can also enjoy looking for animal tracks while sledding through the newly fallen snow.

If it's not possible to have a living tree, visit a tree farm where you can tag and cut your own Christmas tree. It often becomes a hallowed family tradition to go to the tree farm in fall to choose and tag a tree, and then return a week or two before Christmas to cut it down. Tree farms often have a selection of several varieties, in a range of sizes and shapes (see Christmas Trees, page 120). Some tree farms will also ship fresh trees by mail. Either way, you'll get a much fresher and more fragrant tree than if you bought one from a neighborhood lot.

SENSORY PLEASURES: WINTER'S TOUCH

We tend to bundle up and neglect our sense of touch in the winter, in our efforts to protect ourselves from the cold. But we often suffer from a bit of sensory deprivation in the winter as a result. Take off your mittens for a few minutes and reconnect with the world. Savor:

- The dewy feel of snowflakes melting on warm skin

- The cool wind and weightless acceleration of sledding down a hill

- The chilled cheeks of a child's bright face

- The feathery boughs of a fresh evergreen

- The perfect slick smoothness of an icicle

- The soft crunch underfoot as you walk through the snow, or swish your arms and legs in it to make an angel

- The embrace of a warm fire, coming in from the cold

SUGAR ON SNOW

A new snow means it's time for a sweet treat: maple syrup on snow. Gather a bowl of freshly fallen snow from an area you know has not been frequented by animals or people. Heat 4 cups of pure maple syrup in a pan, stirring occasionally, until it reaches 235° to 240°F., the soft-ball stage (use a candy thermometer). Ladle the syrup over bowls of freshly fallen snow or shaved ice. Serve immediately.

Makes 8 servings

HOME FOR THE HOLIDAYS Christmas, in addition to its religious significance, is also a celebration of nature—a time when evergreens, pinecones, and colorful berries can be gathered and fashioned into welcoming wreaths, elegant garlands, and jubilant bouquets to transport color and fragrance indoors. Moss and ferns, pinecones and pods, seashells and stones gathered throughout the year can be fashioned into ornaments and decorations, garnishing presents and homes. Holiday preparations are a wonderful opportunity for families to spend time together, foraging for greens and pinecones in the woods, making wreaths, or baking cookies.

A Christmas inspired by nature can include, but isn't limited to, finds from the forests. You can use almost anything for inspiration. For starters, here are three very different Christmas schemes: an old-fashioned red-and-green woodland Christmas; a white and airy seashore-themed celebration; and a sophisticated silver-polished take on the holidays.

A WOODLAND CELEBRATION The traditional colors of Christmas—red and green—were probably derived from the evergreens and holly berries that bring life to the winter landscape. Celebrate an all-natural Christmas using branches and leaves, berries, and cones brought indoors to brighten winter nights.

A woodland Christmas begins with an outing to collect nature's most brilliant trimmings: vibrant red *staghorn sumac* can be gathered from October through December in meadows and along road

sides. Fresh *moss* continues to grow green under the snow and around the base of forest trees. *Mountain laurel,* a green leafy shrub related to bay leaf, adds a spicy scent to wreaths, garlands, and potpourri, while a mixture of *pinecones* and *pods* can be made into ornaments, centerpieces, and topiaries. Wild *cranberries* are abundant in bog areas, but should be purchased from a store to preserve natural habitats for wildlife.

PINECONE TOPIARY

A large sugar pinecone becomes a dramatic topiary nestled in an old champagne bucket. Cut a piece of florists' foam to fit the container, then anchor the base of the cone into the foam. Fill with fresh greenery to cover the foam.

THE HOLIDAY TABLE

A natural scheme adds rich color and texture while keeping the mood casually festive. A red tablecloth is angled across a turn-of-the-century farm table, with a wooden plank serving as a runner for candlesticks, vases, and pinecone and cranberry balls. Matte green Art Deco pottery from the 1930s is filled with berries and nuts. At the center is a filbert topiary made by hot-gluing hazelnuts and sprigs of reindeer moss to a papier-mâché cone.

NATURAL CHRISTMAS BALLS

Balls—to use as ornaments or as decorations—can be covered with cranberries, small pinecones, acorns, or leaves. To make, start with papier-mâché balls (available at crafts stores) as a base. Using a hot-glue gun, apply glue to one section of the ball at a time, then affix berries, cones, or desired elements to the ball to completely cover the surface. Here, glass cake stands in graduated sizes, collected at tag sales and antiques shops, are stacked one upon another, to hold an array of cranberry and pinecone balls nestled in ferns and mountain laurel leaves. The crowning touch: a martini glass holding a cranberry sphere.

RIGHT Each place at the table is set with a beige buffalo china plate, an antique amber wineglass, and a linen napkin decorated with a pressed autumn leaf. BELOW A centerpiece tableau mixes fresh-cut evergreens with pressed fern fronds and autumn leaves, sumac berries, acorns, and hazelnuts. A pillar candle is studded with cranberries, which have been affixed with straight pins. As the candle burns, the berries cast a festive glow. Flat-bottomed cones are called into service as place card holders—just tuck a card into the cone's crown.

This section is designed as a reference guide for your explorations into nature, as well as a journal in which to record your own discoveries. You may also want to bring a color-illustrated guide to plants, wildflowers, and trees to help you learn what you're looking at, and to identify any poisonous or endangered plants. Beyond that, common sense is your best guide.

BEING PREPARED

CLOTHING

In spring, the ground is likely to be soggy with runoff from melting snow and rising streams. Wear rubber boots to keep your feet dry and protected. Layer clothing—a T-shirt, a sweatshirt or sweater, and a jacket or windbreaker—so you'll be comfortable but able to shed layers as the day gets warmer. Protect exposed skin with a tick-and-insect repellent.

For summertime expeditions, clothing should be lightweight and loose fitting to allow your skin to breathe. Wear a light, long-sleeved shirt, long pants, and a wide-brimmed hat to protect yourself from mosquitoes, black flies, deer ticks, and sun exposure. If walking along the beach or in an open meadow, protect exposed skin with tick-and-insect repellent and full-spectrum sunscreen. Lightweight shoes with rugged soles will protect your feet from sharp rocks, roots, and glass. Sturdy waterproof sandals or shoes such as Tevas or Aqua Socks can help protect your feet on the beach or in the water.

In autumn, as in spring, it's a good idea to layer clothes in order to be able to adjust to changing temperatures. Work or hiking boots will give your feet support for ascending a ridge to view the autumn foliage.

Winter walks require a little more preparation. A hat that covers the ears, gloves or mittens, and a scarf are essential for protection from the cold temeratures and falling snow. In below-freezing temperatures, wear long underwear (polypropylene, Capilene, or silk is best) and layer on a turtleneck, a sweater, and a wool shirt or polar fleece pullover beneath a windproof jacket. Well-insulated, waterproof boots are a must; you may want to add thermal liners as well.

SAFETY

While being outdoors is about enjoying all that nature has to offer, there are some precautions you should take and potentially dangerous situations you should avoid:

1 Never come in contact with an animal that is hurt or seems to be disoriented. Wild animals can carry diseases such as rabies.

2 Be aware that in spring and summer, rivers and streams can overflow rapidly due to rainwater and snow runoff, causing flash floods and rough currents. Avoid danger by checking the water level and flow from a distance.

3 When collecting seashells, be aware of the incoming or outgoing tide and the strength of the undertow. Strong ocean currents can throw you off balance.

4 If caught in a lightning storm, seek shelter immediately.

5 In winter, check the temperature and the wind chill factor and dress appropriately to avoid frostbite.

6 Woods can be dangerous during hunting season. Be cautious when in woodland areas frequented by hunters and wear a highly visible "hunter's orange" vest or jacket when venturing into the forest.

POISONOUS AND ENDANGERED PLANTS

Always carry an illustrated guidebook with you in order to correctly identify any poisonous or endangered plants. Never eat anything without knowing for certain that it is safe. Also, be aware that some wild plants may be considered endangered in one state and not in another, so consult with your local forestry bureau before picking.

Plants that Cause Skin Irritation and Rashes

POISON IVY

POISON OAK

POISON SUMAC

Poisonous Plants, Nuts, and Berries

FOXGLOVE

LUPINE

BUTTERCUP

HORSE CHESTNUTS

VIRGINIA CREEPER

SORBUS

DUCHESNEA (mock strawberries)

MUSHROOMS (Wild fungi can be eaten only if definitively identified.)

Endangered Plants and Wildflowers

This varies from state to state. Call your state's Department of Forestry for an up-to-date listing.

COLLECTING AND PRESERVING NATURE

COLLECTING KIT

Keep the tools you need for gathering wildflowers, branches, shells, and berries handy—either in your car or to take with you on walks, so you're always prepared for excursions.

CAR KIT

When you're driving through the countryside, you may come across interesting items unexpectedly. Keep a collecting kit in the car at all times so you can gather an impromptu bouquet of wildflowers or a colorful selection of autumn leaves.

In a strong but lightweight basket, assemble:

- A guidebook on plants, wildflowers, and trees

- Bug and tick repellent

- Sharp garden scissors and pruning shears

- A book for pressing ferns and leaves

- 2 liters of spring water to keep wildflowers and foliage hydrated

- Several aluminum cans for holding flowers or branches

The basket itself can be used to gather pinecones, seashells, stones, pods, and berries.

WALKING KIT

A walk on the beach or a hike through the woods can offer a multitude of opportunities for collecting. Keep your hands free and wear a backpack outfitted with:

- A guidebook on plants and flowers, or one detailing sea life and shells

- Binoculars to view animals and birds from a distance

- A small magnifying glass to study detail on shells and stones, lichen, moss, bark, or plants

- A nylon or net bag that folds up easily but can expand to hold shells, pinecones, pods, or rocks

- An extra water bottle with a wide mouth to hold flowers and foliage (always keep a water bottle filled for drinking as well)

FERNS

Cut ferns early in the morning, when the temperature is coolest. Cut stems on an angle with a sharp knife and place directly into a bucket of tepid water. Once home, submerge ferns in a tub of cool water for twenty-four hours before arranging.

Types of Woodland Ferns

LADY FERN	OAK FERN
HAY-SCENTED FERN	SENSITIVE FERN
MALE FERN	CINNAMON FERN
NORTHERN MAIDENHAIR FERN	CHRISTMAS FERN
	ROYAL FERN

Ferns for Cutting

HAY-SCENTED FERN	BRACKEN FERN
MAIDENHAIR FERN	SWEET FERN
BAMBOO FERN	

FORCING BRANCHES

Using a sharp knife or pruning shears, cut branches on an angle just above the nub where an offshoot would sprout. Place branches directly into lukewarm water. Once home, smash stems with a hammer and plunge in hot water for ten seconds, then in cold water. Place in a clean vase or container filled with a solution of half water and half tonic water and keep in a cool spot.

Trees Suitable for Forcing

BIRCH	ELM
OAK	ALDER
BEECH	PUSSY WILLOWS
MAPLE	

WILDFLOWERS

Cut flowers early in the morning after the dew has dried from the blossoms. Place in a clean pail of tepid water and let stand for several hours before arranging. Strip any leaves that will fall below the waterline, recut stems, and place in a vase with a solution of $\frac{1}{4}$ cup sugar, 1 tablespoon bleach, and an aspirin tablet for every gallon of water.

Wildflowers for Cutting

CLOVER	QUEEN ANNE'S LACE
PEARLY EVERLASTING	WILD PHLOX
GOLDENROD	COW VETCH
DAISIES	WHITE YARROW
LUPINE	BUTTERCUPS
INDIAN PAINTBRUSH	BLACK-EYED SUSAN

COLLECTING SEEDS

Collecting seeds from wildflowers and grasses to add to your garden or landscape is a process that must be planned ahead of time for the best results. To collect seeds, gently crush dried flower blossoms over a brown envelope to expose and catch seeds. For plumes of grass, run fingers down the plume, stripping the seedpods from the stalk. In most cases, flowers admired in the wild are at their peak of blossoming, which also means their seeds are immature and will probably yield poor results. For the best results:

1 Tag plants or make notes on the locations of wildflowers from which you collect seeds so you can monitor the plants' progress.

2 As the blossoms fade and die, the flower or grass will dry, exposing the seeds or forming a seedpod. Wait until the flower or seedpod has fully dried before harvesting.

3 When choosing seedpods, compare different ones you've collected to find the most mature ones. Mature seed casings should be hard and difficult to break. Large seedpods, like those found on the lupine plant, often dry and pop, spreading their own seeds into the wild. Try to collect seeds from pods as late as possible but before the pods break. For best results, collect pods right before they open and then continue drying on a flat screen in a dry place.

4 Check drying blossoms frequently, and collect seeds from pods or flowers at several different times to help insure that at least some of the seeds in your collection have reached full maturity.

5 Collect a large number of seeds; as many as fifty seeds per square foot will be necessary for successful propagation.

6 Store dried blossoms, seeds, and seedpods in a dry area in paper envelopes marked with species and location information.

7 To plant, spread seeds over fertile ground before the ground becomes hardened with frost, or early in spring after the ground has thawed.

Wildflowers for Gardens

DAISIES	COW VETCH
LUPINE	PHLOX
BLACK-EYED SUSAN	CLOVER
BUTTERCUPS	

AUTUMN LEAVES

Gather leaves that have already fallen and place them between the pages of a book. Or cut branches in the same manner described for forcing branches (see page 116).

The Most Colorful Autumn Leaves

SUGAR, SILVER, AND RED MAPLE	COPPER BEECH
	OAK
YELLOW AND WHITE BIRCH	ASH
BEECH	HICKORY

BERRIES

When gathering berried branches, wrap heavily berried boughs in newsprint or tissue paper to protect the fruit. Cut and preserve as you would other branches.

Decorative Berries

MARSH BERRIES	ELDERBERRIES
SUMAC BERRIES	VIBURNUM
BITTERSWEET BERRIES	HAWTHORN
	PYRACANTHA
WILD ROSE HIPS	

EVERGREENS

Cut branches in cool weather using pruning shears. Place in water and store in a cool spot until needed.

Fragrant Cut Evergreens

BLUE SPRUCE	HEMLOCK
NOBLE FIR	CEDAR
SCOTCH PINE	JUNIPER

PINECONES

Use a large basket or sturdy bag to collect pinecones. They require no special care and will last forever.

Types of Cones

PINE	SCOTCH
WHITE	MOUNTAIN
PITCH	BALSAM FIR
SWAMP	HEMLOCK
LOBLOLLY	SPRUCE
LONGLEAF	BLACK
SHORTLEAF	RED
RED	WHITE
JACK	NORWAY
SCRUB	

DRYING METHODS

PRESSING

Place items between the pages of a book weighted with a brick or heavy rock, or use a flower press. This method is suitable for:

LEAVES such as maple, oak, chestnut, birch, laurel

FERNS

FLOWERS if their heads are not too thick

SCREEN DRYING

Place items on a large window screen or other framed piece of screening, which has been propped up on books or chairs to allow air to circulate freely. This method is best for:

MOSS

PINECONES

ACORNS

PODS

NUTS

SEASHELLS

AIR DRYING

Flowers with large blossoms can often be joined together in bouquets, then hung upside down with cord or raffia from a beam or shelf and allowed to air-dry naturally.

SEASIDE COLLECTIBLES

Gather seashells and other oceanside collectibles in lightweight wire baskets or fabric mesh bags that can easily be run under clean water to remove sand and salt spray. Dry flat on a screen in an arid place to eliminate any strong seaside odors.

SEA GLASS

SEASHELLS

STARFISH

SAND DOLLARS

DRIFTWOOD

BEACH STONES

CHRISTMAS TREES

Select your tree a couple of weeks before Christmas, when there are still a lot to choose from. Be sure to choose a healthy tree that will survive the holiday season.

Types of Trees

SPRUCE This full, bushy conical-shaped tree has a handsome appearance but loses its needles quickly.

BLUE SPRUCE Dense bluish green needles (somewhat tough and prickly) on well-spaced branches make this tree preferred by many ornament aficionados.

NORWAY SPRUCE The slightly drooping branches of Norway spruces have an elegant shape but are hard to decorate.

SCOTCH PINE A full, rounded pine tree with clusters of needles and pointed cones, the Scotch pine is generally shorter and wider than a spruce or a fir, and they tend to have the best needle retention.

EASTERN WHITE PINE This tree has bunches of long, soft, bright green needles with a full, lush overall shape and a mild fragrance. Ornaments can be tucked in among its branches more easily than hung.

BALSAM FIR One of the most popular Christmas trees, tall and steeple shaped, with slender branching and light green needles. Firs have excellent needle retention, and Balsam firs, in particular, are very fragrant.

FRASER FIR This fir has short, soft, dark green needles, a pleasing symmetrical shape, and good fragrance.

HEMLOCK Not typically used as a Christmas tree because of its thin and wispy branches, a hemlock nonetheless makes a pretty silhouette if left undecorated; silver-green foliage and small brown cones; should be left up only for a week or two because it sheds its needles so quickly.

Caring for a Christmas Tree

- When selecting a tree, bend its needles to test for freshness. A freshly cut tree's needles will be supple and malleable; a tree past its prime will feel dry and needles will shed and break at the touch.

- Bounce the tree on the base of its trunk. Any tree will lose a few needles, but it shouldn't start raining needles.

- Recut the tree immediately on returning home. Remove at least an inch from the end of the trunk with a handsaw and plunge into a bucket of water. Let stand in a cool, but not freezing, spot for several hours.

- Place the tree in a tree stand with a large water reservoir. Trees do best in cooler areas—65° to 68°F.—so spots near windows or doors are usually good. Keep away from fireplaces or radiators, which will rapidly dry out needles. Refill water daily or as needed—trees tend to drink a lot of water, particularly during the first day.

- Recycle your tree after the holiday season by donating to a community program that will turn it into nutrient-rich mulch for flower beds and gardens.

SEASONAL NOTES AND OBSERVATIONS

SPRING

What Found and Where

SUMMER

What Found and Where

FLOWERING
TREES _____

WILDFLOWERS _____

_____

_____

_____

_____

_____

WILDFLOWERS _____

_____

_____

_____

_____

_____

BERRIES AND
FORAGING _____

_____

FORAGING _____

_____

_____

_____

_____

_____

_____

AUTUMN

What Found and Where

COLORFUL
TREES _____

_____

_____

BERRIES _____

_____

_____

WILDFLOWERS _____

_____

_____

_____

FORAGING _____

_____

_____

_____

WINTER

What Found and Where

EVERGREENS _____

_____

_____

CONES _____

_____

_____

BERRIES _____

_____

_____

_____

NATURAL PRODUCTS AND HOME ACCESSORIES

ECO DESIGN
1365 Rufina Circle
Santa Fe, NM 87505
800-621-2591
Call or write for the catalog titled "The Natural Choice." Natural and nontoxic paints, stains, and other products.

THE NATURE COMPANY
PO Box 188
Florence, KY 41022
800-227-1114
Call or write for a catalog of nature-inspired products or the nearest store location.

TERRA VERDE TRADING CO.
120 Wooster Street
New York, NY 10012
212-925-4533
Retail store of natural products and accessories.

DRIED MEADOW FLOWERS, GRASSES, SEASONAL BERRIES, PODS AND CONES, FRESH EVERGREEN

ATTAR
21 Playground Road
New Ipswich, NH 03071
603-878-1780
Natural essential oils, orrisroot, and dried botanicals. Call for wholesale catalog ($50.00 minimum) or nearest retailer.

FANCY'S FARM
PO Box 98
199 Main Street
East Orleans, MA 02643
508-255-1949

FREDRICKSBURG HERB FARM
PO Drawer 927
Fredricksburg, TX 78624-0972
800-259-4372
Mail order, newsletter, and herbal products.

THE GAVELSTON WREATH CO.
1124 25th Street
Gavelston, TX 77550-4409
409-765-8597
Wreath forms, dried meadow grasses, and flowers.

JBC TREE FARM
800-540-3391
Call for a selection of freshly cut and shipped evergreen boughs, wreaths, and Christmas trees.

KNUD NIELSEN CO.
800-698-5656
Dried leaves, berries, wildflowers, and moss. Call for nearest retailer.

LAND OF THE SKY NURSERIES
108 Lakewood Drive
Asheville, NC 28803
Write for a catalog of pinecones, pods, and berries.

SHELLS AND STARFISH

LOOSE ENDS
503-390-7457
Seashells, scallop shells, and starfish. Call for nearest retailer.

SANIBEL SEASHELL INDUSTRIES
905 Fitzhugh Street
Sanibel Island, FL 33957
941-472-1603
Call or write for a wide selection of shells and starfish.

SHE SELLS SEASHELLS
1157 Periwinkle Way
Sanibel Island, FL 33957
941-472-6991
Call or write for shells, starfish coral, and other beach finds.

THE SHELL CELLAR
89 South Street
South Street Seaport Pier 17
New York, NY 10038
212-962-1076
Mail order for shells and preserved sea life. Call for other locations.

RIBBONS, TRIMS, AND TWINES

HYMAN HENDLER AND SONS
67 West 38th Street
New York, NY 10018
212-840-8393
Imported silk and satin ribbons.

LOOSE ENDS
See above ("Shells and Starfish")
Complete line of recycled papers, natural rope, and twine.

SO-GOOD INC.
28 West 38th Street
New York, NY 10018
212-398-0236
Satin, grosgrains, velvet, and
taffeta ribbons.

TINSEL TRADING
47 West 38th Street
New York, NY 10018
212-730-1030
Ribbons, trims, and twines.

CRAFT MATERIALS AND SUPPLIES

DOROTHY BIDDLE FLOWER
SUPPLY
HC01, Box 900
Greeley, PA 18425
717-226-3239
Call or write for a catalog of
supplies. Glycerin, florist wire,
wreath frames.

THE LAMP SHOP
PO Box 3606
Concord, NH 03302-3606
Write for a catalog of lamp parts
and shade supplies.

METALIFEROUS
34 West 46th Street
New York, NY 10036
212-944-0909
Call or send $4.00 for a catalog
of aluminum wire, screening,
and copper mesh.

ACCESSORIES, TOOLS, AND CONTAINERS

BROOKSTONE COMPANY
1655 Bassford Drive
Mexico, MO 65265
800-846-3000
Binoculars, compasses, and
pruning shears.

CLAPPER'S
1125 Washington Street
West Newton, MA 02165
617-244-7909
Cast aluminum and concrete
urns and pots.

EASTERN MOUNTAIN
SPORTS
603-924-9571
Wide selection of outdoor clothing and nature guidebooks. Call
for nearest store location.

SMITH AND HAWKEN
25 Corte Madera
Mill Valley, CA 94941
800-776-3336
Call for a seasonal catalog of
gifts, tools, and accessories.

PARKS, PRESERVES, AND BOTANICAL GARDENS

BIRMINGHAM BOTANICAL
GARDENS
2612 Lane Park Road
Birmingham, AL 35223
205-879-1227

BOWMAN'S HILL
WILDFLOWER PRESERVE
Box 103, River Road
Washington Crossing, PA 18977
215-862-2924

BROOKLYN BOTANIC
GARDENS
1000 Washington Avenue
Brooklyn, NY 11225
718-622-4433

FERNWOOD BOTANIC
GARDENS
13988 Range Line Road
Niles, MI 49120
616-695-6491

GARDEN IN THE WOODS
AT THE NEW ENGLAND
WILDFLOWER SOCIETY
180 Hemenway Road
Framingham, MA 01701-2699
617-237-4924
Grounds open from April 15 to
October 31.

THE MARIE SELBY
BOTANICAL GARDENS
811 South Palm Avenue
Sarasota, FL 33577
813-366-5731

THE NEW YORK
BOTANICAL GARDEN
Southern Boulevard
Bronx, NY 10458
718-817-8705

U.S. NATIONAL ARBORETUM
3501 New York Avenue N.E.
Washington, DC 20002
202-475-4815

UNIVERSITY OF CALIFORNIA
BOTANICAL GARDEN
AT BERKELEY
Centennial Drive
Berkeley, CA 94729
510-643-8040

SOCIETIES AND PRESERVATION GROUPS

AMERICAN FERN SOCIETY
456 McGill Place
Atlanta, GA 30312
Please write for information.

BIRMINGHAM FERN SOCIETY
Birmingham Botanic Gardens
2612 Lane Park Road
Birmingham, AL 35223
205-879-1227

DELAWARE VALLEY FERN
+ WILDFLOWER SOCIETY
1030 Limekiln Pike
Maple Glen, PA 19002

LOS ANGELES
INTERNATIONAL FERN
SOCIETY
Box 90943
Pasadena, CA 91109-0943
Please write for information.

NATIONAL AUDUBON
SOCIETY
700 Broadway
New York, NY 10003-9562
212-979-3000

NATIONAL WILDFLOWER
RESEARCH CENTER
4801 La Crosse Boulevard
Austin, TX 78739
512-292-4200

THE NATURE CONSERVANCY
1815 North Lynn Street
Arlington, VA 22209
703-841-5300

NEW ENGLAND
WILDFLOWER SOCIETY
180 Hemenway Road
Framingham, MA 01701-2699
617-237-4924

SOUTHWESTERN
FERN SOCIETY
515 S. Lois Lane
Richardson, TX 75081
Please write for information.

RETAIL AND MAIL-ORDER SUPPLIERS

FERNS
These nurseries offer live ferns
by mail.

FANCY FRONDS/
FARFOD'S HARDY FERNS
1911 Fourth Avenue West
Seattle, WA 98119
206-284-5332
Catalog, $2

KURT BLUEMEL, INC.
2740 Breene Lane
Baldwin, MD 21013-9523
410-557-7229
Catalog, $3

SUNLIGHT GARDENS
174 Olden Lane
Andersonville, TN 37705
615-494-8237
Catalog, $3

WHITE FLOWER FARM
30 Irene Street
Torrington, CT 06790
800-411-6159
Mail-order ferns, lupine, and
wildflowers. Call for a catalog
and retail locations.

WILDFLOWER SEED MIXTURES

BOTANIC GARDEN
SEED CO., INC.
9 Wykoff Street
Brooklyn, NY 11202
718-624-8839

ENVIRONMENTAL SEED
PRODUCTS
PO Box 5904
El Monte, CA 91734
818-442-3330
Will create custom mixes.

PASSIFLORA WILDFLOWERS
Route 1, Box 190-A
Germantown, NC 27019
919-591-5816
Will create custom mixes.

THE WILDFLOWER
SEED COMPANY
800-456-3359
Call for a catalog.

Recommended Reading

The Audubon Society Field Guide Series: NORTH AMERICAN SHELLS, TREES (EASTERN AND WESTERN), WILDFLOWERS (EASTERN AND WESTERN) (New York: Alfred A. Knopf, 1981).

FIELD GUIDE TO EDIBLE WILD PLANTS, by Bradford Angier (Harrisburg, Penn.: Stackpole Books, 1994).

FIELD GUIDE TO EDIBLE WILD PLANTS, by Lee Allen Peterson (Boston: Houghton Mifflin, 1977).

THE HISTORY AND FOLKLORE OF NORTH AMERICAN WILDFLOWERS, by Timothy Coffey (Boston: Houghton Mifflin, 1993).

The National Audubon Society Pocket Guide Series: FAMILIAR FLOWERS OF NORTH AMERICA (EASTERN AND WESTERN), TREES (EASTERN AND WESTERN) (New York: Chanticleer Press, Alfred A. Knopf, 1986).

Stokes Nature Guides: NATURE IN WINTER, by Donald Stokes (Boston: Little, Brown, 1976).

TOM BROWN'S FIELD GUIDE TO NATURE OBSERVATION AND TRACKING, by Tom Brown Jr. (New York: Berkley Books, 1983).

VANISHING FLORA, by Dugald Stermer (New York: Harry N. Abrams, 1995).

WILDFLOWERS ACROSS AMERICA, by Lady Bird Johnson and Carlton B. Lees (New York: Abbeville Press, 1988).

Rare and Antique Books

THE FERN COLLECTOR'S GUIDE, by Willard N. Clute (London: Frederick A. Stokes Co., 1902).

FERNS AND HOW TO GROW THEM, by G. A. Woolson (New York: Doubleday, Page and Co., 1905).

FERNS OF NORTHEASTERN UNITED STATES (New York: The American Museum of Natural History, 1936).

GETTING ACQUAINTED WITH THE TREES, by J. Horace McFarland (New York: The Outlook Co., 1904).

HOW TO KNOW THE WILDFLOWERS, by Mrs. William Starr Dana (New York: Charles Scribner's Sons, 1893).

OUR NATIVE TREES, by Harriet L. Keeler (New York: Charles Scribner's Sons, 1904).

TREE GUIDE, by Julia Ellen Rogers (New York: Doubleday, Page and Co., 1922).

WHERE TO FIND FERNS, by Francis George Heath (London: E. & J. B. Young and Co., 1885).

WILD FLOWERS OF AMERICA, by Jane Harvey (New York: Whitman Publishing Co., 1932).